Rose Quartz Symphonies

Lola D.

BookLeaf
Publishing

Presentation by *BookLeaf Publishing*

Web: www.bookleafpub.com

E-mail: info@bookleafpub.com

ISBN: 9789357695947

First edition 2022

*To my lifetime partner, the love of my life,
the man of my dreams and the most
miraculous blessing that God has ever
given me.*

ACKNOWLEDGEMENT

First and foremost, I am giving thanks to Bookleaf Publishing. This book would not be in existence without you all; I truly appreciate each and every single one of you.

Next, I am thanking my beloved- you know who you are! Without you, I would never have known a love so tender, genuine and forgiving. A love that tastes of honey, smells of cinnamon and blazes fire within my heart. A love that sings sweet and mellow symphonies during Spring, Summer, Fall and Winter. And, a love that shines beyond the galaxy. Thank you for such a worthy love!

Following, I would like to give thanks to any and everyone who helped make this book possible. You all are abundantly appreciated! I could not have done this on my own.

Lastly, I am grateful and thankful to God Almighty for allowing these words to flow out of me and giving my life so much love.

PREFACE

When I think about being in love, only one person comes to my mind, heart, soul and spirit. I'm head over heels in love with my soulmate, my knight in shining armor and better half.

This is a series of Haiku that captures the love I have for my lifeline and celebrates the birth of our fifth-year anniversary.

Happy Fifth Anniversary to My Forevermore!

Jungle Fever

Jaguar and lion.
Pain, tears, rain, storms, hurricanes,
can't stop our wildin.

Halloween

My Littmus Lozenge.
My bittersweet, trick or treat.
Will you be my Jack?

Sun of Saturn

A starry-blazing
love too unconditional
for this universe.

New Moon

Beginnings, endings.
When did our souls intersect?
Capricorn's Leo.

Spring's Song

5

The trees' laughter rings.
As you bless me with a kiss,
I can hear Spring sing.

Chinquapin Seed

Gateways to the past.
Our first experiences,
so picture perfect.

Coitus' Bouquet

Love molds our bodies
as our limbs become tangled-
roses fly, thorns lie.

The Moonwalk

The stars dance with us.
As our auras intertwine,
The moon starts to wink.

Lifetime Lover

He's my tender-world.
He's my sunrise, my sunset.
He's who parts my sea.

Be Mine

Will you be my knight?
Will you be my kids' father
and always my king?

Love Story

Our love is genius.
Our love is so genuine.
Our love's generous.

Spicy Hearts

Cinnamon charcoal.
Ignition of red chili.
Wood chips of ginger.

The Kisses of Kenya

Dark, bottomless eyes,
smooth cheeks, luscious lips, rich smiles.
Celestial kisses.

Forevermore

Wine, honey, glucose.
Infinite warp, black hole.
Supernova heat.

Union

Leaves fall, flowers bloom.
The wind caresses the Earth
as our souls combine.

August in December

Blue lava hearts fuse
in the Summer and Winter.
Such a cosmic love.

The Crack of Dawn

Passionate mornings.
Bed-rocking to a bird's call.
Wild cats are purring.

Twilight

Darkness falls and finds
us, Sun and Moon aligned
as climates entwine.

Black Diamond

You're waves to my heat.
You're fire and desire.
You're my black diamond.

The Art of Us

Pen to my paper.
Oil pastel to my canvas.
The brush to my paint.

Super Zario Brother

You sailor my moon,
caption my anime, then
super my saiyan.